I0203206

when souls take flight

take

flight

Coping with Grief

Kira Rosner

COHERENT BOOKS

When Souls Take Flight

First Edition

Copyright © 2008 Kira Rosner

All rights reserved. No part of this publication may be reproduced, stored in a retrieval system, or transmitted by any form, electronic, mechanical, photocopying, recording or otherwise, except for the inclusion of brief quotations in a review or article, without written permission from the publisher or author.

Published by Coherent Books: www.KiraRosner.com

ISBN: 978-0-9679978-2-7
LCCN: 2007908626

Book Interior by Kira Rosner: www.KiraRosner.com
Cover Design by Mitchell Maisel: 954.295.0164

Printed and Distributed by Lightning Source Inc.
www.LightningSource.com

Publisher's Cataloging-In-Publication Data
(Prepared by The Donohue Group, Inc.)

Rosner, Kira.
When souls take flight: coping with grief/Kira Rosner. -- 1st ed.

p. ; cm.

ISBN: 978-0-9679978-2-7

1. Death. 2. Future life. 3. Ascension of the soul. 4. Grief.
5. Bereavement. 6. Metaphysics. I. Title.

BD444 .R67 2007
155.9/37   2007908626

Dedicated to the memory of
those who have passed.
Our love lives on.

Contents

Your soul is lit from within, and that light
is a spark of divinity shining through you.

My Father's Wings

I came face to face with death when I witnessed my beloved father's passage. As his breath grew labored, I sensed a change coming. The air became soft and luminous. I had never felt anything like it. The entire room was aglow, textured with a lively silence.

My family and I were glued to the rise and fall of dad's chest as we called out parting words of love. It reminded me of being on a train platform shouting farewells as the train pulled away from the station.

Except when my father's breathing stilled, he was neither out of sight nor hearing range. The only thing he was out of was his body. He was above it. Ethereal. Translucent. The instant I saw him, I felt his surprise and awe. He was free and out of pain.

In what seemed like seconds, the picture shifted. He was off to the side floating up a large golden cone of light. It was exactly as if someone were shining a giant flashlight directly through the ceiling. It was warm. Radiant. Beckoning.

Then suddenly, he paused in mid-flight. I looked more closely and could see that the sight of those crying around his body anchored him. Silently, with a strength I didn't know I possessed, I assured him we would take care of one another.

With that sentiment, he let go of whatever hold he had and gently rose upward, disappearing from view as the light enveloped him. All that remained was the certainty he was on his way home.

Since that night, I have known with perfect clarity that death is a blessed and reverent event. While it may be challenging for those of us left behind, we can take comfort in the knowledge our loved ones are safely ashore.

Inner Light

If I asked you to describe yourself, many of you would describe your appearance and personality. It is helpful to realize that we are more than bodies with likes and dislikes. We are strong, complex beings with a wealth of intricate layers. Some of those layers are obvious; others are hidden from view. Combined, they create the people we are today.

At the core of our being is a vital force which is integral to our existence. This essence is "our soul." Our souls play an important role in our lives, yet I have observed something. Although our thoughts span a wide range of subjects on any given day, we seem to reserve the topic of souls for funerals and special occasions.

For example, when we attend memorial services, we feel reassured hearing that the soul of our loved one has departed. I agree. It is comforting to hear that someone we love has made a smooth transition.

3

What I would like to know is: Where were our souls when we were eating breakfast this morning?

If the soul departs when someone dies, that implies it is leaving, right? Think it over. It had to be somewhere before it left, didn't it? We don't leave the house unless we were in the house to begin with.

Overall, we are a very bright species. Yet some of us fail to appreciate how multidimensional we are. We seem to have more awareness of the soul's departure when we die, than of its presence when we are very much alive.

We Are Souls

To expand our understanding, let's talk about the soul's arrival and departure. We often call these events the beginning and end of life, as we know it. By "as we know it," I am referring to conventional views on birth and death.

We will start with how our soul and body meet. When a new infant is conceived, our physiology is gracefully knit from the genetic material of both our mother and father. Next, our soul alights, forging an intimate mystical bond with our body. We could call it a spiritual marriage. The lightness of our soul is wed to the density of our physical form. Together we inhale our first breath of oxygen.

I say "our" because it's a partnership between spirit and flesh – living and learning and loving in unison.

Now that we have discussed how our soul and body meet, what happens when they part?

What do you think happens when we die? Do you think we remain in our lifeless bodies waving goodbye to our souls as they depart?

I will repeat the question in more detail. Do you think we remain in our lifeless bodies, our cognitive abilities diminishing until we black out entirely like a light switch the cosmic electrician has turned off, and the last memory any of us have is waving goodbye to our souls?

Given a choice, wouldn't you be more inclined to go with your soul and see where it's going? I know I would.

Our souls are an inseparable part of who we are. They are with us in birth, throughout our lifespan on Earth, and our passage beyond. When they depart, we go with them. Why? Because we are souls.

As the breath stills and the connection between the soul and body is released, it will become crystal clear. We will realize we are renters, not owners. You could call us the tenants. When our homes can no longer house us, we vacate the premises.

Or, we could say the premises vacate us in a defining moment that completes our body's journey and initiates our soul's journey. I'll explain what I mean.

When our heart is beating, our soul's life force and our body's life force go hand in hand like best friends. We can compare their friendship to two bi-cyclists riding tandem through life.

When our body retires, everything changes. Our union comes to an amiable split, and the mystical bond that I spoke of works in reverse. Instead of the merging we experienced when we aligned with our body, we feel a disconnect, a separation, a release...

It's effortless, similar to a swish off air. At this point, we spontaneously reclaim our original form as a soul or *light body*. Conscious, alert, with our life force fully intact, we are free to function on our own.

So you see, we are more than our physical bodies. We are immortal souls joined in holy matrimony to mortal bodies. That is what I call creative wedding planning.

Eternity outshines the illusion of mortality.

Homecoming

Where do our souls go when we depart? Just as those who have departed before us, we go to a celestial realm, where we are nourished and renewed and reunited with other light beings like ourselves. There eternity outshines the illusion of mortality.

Aren't we mortal? Physically, we are. But souls are not physical. They are metaphysical.

Meta means beyond. Metaphysical implies that souls exist beyond standard physical parameters. As such, the laws that govern the physical universe do not apply to our souls. So just because our treasured bodies draw to a close doesn't necessarily mean the ride is over.

This explains why souls have their own views on life and death. On Earth, we're under the impression that our earthly life is real and our soul life is surreal. That is one vantage point.

Souls see it from another angle. They consider their soul life real and their earthly life surreal. To a soul, being human is a temporary stopover, while being a soul is continuous.

Duets

What comes to your mind when you hear the word "soul"? Do you breathe a deep sigh of appreciation at the thought of being a radiant life form engaged in a duet with a human body? Do you rejoice at the affinity you feel living on a planet full of souls engaged in duets with human bodies?

Or does the word "soul" conjure an image of a wispy, dreamlike creature you saw in a painting or stained glass window? And while you might like to think that image had something to do with you, does the chance of your being depicted in that painting seem about as implausible as sprouting wings and flying to the supermarket?

I think many of us are willing to entertain the idea that we have an eternal soul, but are less likely to concede to actually being an eternal soul. We seem more comfortable thinking of ourselves as bodies with souls, than souls with bodies.

Some of us identify with our anatomy so fully, we question whether or not we have a connection to the spiritual realm.

What's your take on it? If bodies are impermanent and souls are everlasting, which one are we?

Heartstrings

Generation after generation, we have equated death with tragedy. Any mention of it is considered morbid. Getting word that someone has died is bad news. Obituaries are dry and serious. Funerals are somber. People wear dark clothing and speak in hushed tones. Mourners cry. Overwhelmed by grief, some of us feel so devastated we have to be sedated in order to cope. Feelings of loss and inconsolable heartache continue for days, weeks, years, even lifetimes.

Is suffering our only option, or is there an alternative? To explore the answer, ask yourself this: When you hear about the death of someone close to you and your eyes pool with tears, is your response instinctive or learned?

What's the difference? An instinctive response is innate, while a learned response is acquired through experience. Some call it a programmed response.

We assume our emotions are instinctive because they feel so close to us, so private. But isn't the way we respond to death triggered by the way we relate to death? And isn't the way we relate to death a by-product of associations we formed growing up?

Consider this: Imagine if your parents had taught you that death was a day of liberation for the soul, explaining that the soul and body have an agreement. As long as the body is alive, they will coexist. Once the body expires, they'll go their separate ways. The body will be laid to rest, and the soul will return to its spiritual home, a place where souls reside with other souls long after their physical bodies cease to function.

Imagine if your parents also taught you about the community that exists among souls. Assuring you from the time you were a young child, that when someone passes from this earth plane, you will see him or her again. Because souls are joined to other souls, the way hearts are joined to other hearts, and love never dies.

Can you see how an upbringing like that would impact the way you relate to death and, therefore, respond?

To varying degrees we are all products of our environment. The fact is, a number of us were raised to associate death with feelings of loss and finality, shrouded by fear and helplessness. Is it any wonder we suffer when someone dies? We are conditioned to believe that death is the end of life.

What is a belief? A belief is an impression from the past that we carry with us into the present. Some people liken them to grooves in our thinking. When we believe something, we repeatedly travel the same mental highways and arrive at the same destination. For this reason, beliefs are called repetitive thinking patterns.

Did you know beliefs have emotional correlates? For example, if we believe death is a dark abyss and we will never see our loved one again, we are likely to feel one way. If we believe that the soul is enjoying a family reunion and we will see our loved ones again, we are likely to feel another. We can compare beliefs to puppeteers pulling our heartstrings.

Let's define "conditioning" as a predictable response to certain stimuli. In this situation, our beliefs are the stimuli. When they're repeated, the emotions we associate with those beliefs tend to follow.

That does not mean our anguish isn't genuine! Our feelings merit the utmost respect regardless of how they are incited.

Nor am I suggesting we won't grieve for those who have gone. However, grieving for someone on a wondrous voyage is not the same as grieving for someone whose flame has been extinguished for all time to come. The former promotes hope. The latter perpetuates gloom and emptiness.

This demonstrates how our mind-set can initiate an emotional response. We may not always be aware of this dynamic, but it plays an influential role in shaping our reality. As I said, we are complex creatures. Part of that complexity involves the way our operating systems interface.

Renewal

Speaking of operating systems, what is the first thing we do with a new computer? We program it. How? We determine what our needs are and install software designed to meet those needs. To stay current, we might buy a program one year and upgrade to a newer version the next.

What if we didn't? What if we kept running the same old programs year after year?

This brings up a more relevant question. What if we relied on computers to run our adult lives using data we entered when we were children? Don't you think we'd benefit from an update? If so, wouldn't it be wise to question beliefs we stored in our cerebral files before our tenth birthday?

We have allowed those beliefs to reign over our feelings, our choices, and our behavior for decades. Why? Because we live under the assumption that everything we believe is true.

Is everything we believe true? Put it this way: We believe everything we believe is true and live our lives accordingly.

When we find ourselves doubting our spiritual origin, there is room for improvement. Perhaps some spring cleaning is in order. Maybe a little freshening up with new ideas.

Correction. Old ideas would probably be more apropos, since knowledge of the soul's longevity has been around longer than we have.

Sensitivity

This talk about being eternal souls may sound unfamiliar. It may sound completely far-fetched. Here is the curious part. On some level, we all know that life is enduring and death is simply another part of living. We may not know it consciously, but we know it.

Once someone passes on, they no longer occupy the physical body. The thought of our loved ones being alive without that tangible expression is a giant stretch for many of us.

Then how do we explain the feelings we have that they are with us? We don't only feel the love we have for them. We feel the love they have for us.

Have we merely convinced ourselves they are nearby because we want to believe it? Or could they be residing on a subtler plane, where they retain the ability to love us from afar? Could the love we feel from them be real?

Ask yourself which feels more truthful. To cling to the idea of death as a tragic ending, or relax with confidence, knowing that a new chapter of your loved one's life has begun?

After seeing the way beliefs can elicit emotional responses, does it surprise you to look to your feelings for guidance? Is there a way for us to feel in the present, as opposed to what we have been conditioned to feel?

Yes, there is. We each have an instinctive sense of what feels truthful and what doesn't, just as we have an instinctive sense of what feels natural and what doesn't.

Can we learn to trust our instincts? We already do, but we are so used to taking direction from our minds – we don't always remember to consult with our inner guidance.

Let's try it now. As you read from page to page, begin to pay attention to how you feel. Do certain ideas ring true? Do you sense an inner nod?

Notice, I am not asking if you believe what you are reading is true. I am asking if you sense what you are reading is true. What is the difference? Beliefs are pre-conceived mental concepts. What we sense comes from communing within.

(In an ideal world, what we believe is true and what we sense is true are the same.)

Sensitivity

Here is a simple equation to follow. When something feels truthful or natural, you are probably on the right track. If it doesn't, consider exploring other avenues until it does.

Another revealing sign is body language. As you read from page to page, notice if you're tightening up or relaxing. Again, which feels more natural?

Would viewing death from another perspective feel natural? Let's find out.

A divine event transpires when someone dies.

Divine Event

One of the most difficult situations we face is coming to terms with someone's passing when it happens unexpectedly, or under baffling or adverse conditions. Along with shock and intense grief, we often struggle to comprehend why these events took place.

Even under extreme circumstances, we have the potential to see things from another perspective. We often change our minds concerning events far less meaningful than this deeply personal one.

Surely it helps to know the facts: A person cannot die without their soul's cooperation. This is why we hear stories about people who survive against impossible odds. For example, the sole survivor of a crash. That person's soul was not ready to leave and was not in agreement. If someone has passed on, their soul was ready to leave and was in agreement. Otherwise they would still be here.

I know how delicate this subject is. We live in an era when lives are lost daily in seemingly senseless ways. The idea that the deceased agreed to take their leave is almost too much for us to comprehend. It may seem inconceivable to our logical minds. We may not like it. We may have a hard time believing or accepting it. But how can we debate it?

We may question our own connection to a power greater than ourselves, but how can we question the soul's connection? When someone dies, a divine event transpires.

Transition

Many of us equate the term divinity with something pure and holy and don't necessarily see ourselves in that light. Isn't it about time we did? Isn't it about time we realized we are spiritual beings, and having a soul is more than a metaphor?

Did you know some cultures don't even have the word "death" in their vocabulary? The word they use is similar to "transition."

Those who have transitioned are a step closer to seeing the bigger picture. They don't have to be convinced they have an eternal soul. They're living proof!

An unbreakable alliance unites all beings.

Togetherness

If our loved ones are enjoying an afterlife in an alternate dimension, do the deceased miss us the way we miss them? Their love may be as compelling as ours, but the pain of separation is not as acute for them. I will explain why.

Separation is something we feel primarily in the physical body. Souls are aware of the unbreakable alliance that unites all living beings. They know they will see their dear ones again, so the impulse to miss someone doesn't grab them quite the same way.

To a soul, the people they care about are an ongoing "part" of their life. It's only on Earth that we perceive ourselves as being "apart" from those who have passed.

Healing is a flowering.
In the garden of your reality,
the buds open when you are ready.

Coping with Grief

L oss can ignite a variety of responses, ranging from mild to debilitating. We may feel angry, or frightened, or confused. We may feel upset, or saddened, or shocked, or traumatized. We may feel abandoned, or even guilty or relieved. We may feel numb and weary. We may feel as though a part of our heart has been torn from our chest, and there is no way to breathe. No way to escape from the pain of being separated from those we love, the pain of disappointment and lost dreams.

Pain is the body's alarm signal, informing us that something is amiss and requires our attention. Let's rephrase that. Informing is far too mild a word. Pain demands attention! One thing is certain. We know we want it to stop.

To go on living with some degree of normalcy and balance, we have to find a way to acclimate to our current situation.

Going on means adjusting, not forgetting. The goal is to hold on to the love without holding on to the pain.

When we are grieving, the two seem indivisible. We cannot feel the love without feeling the pain, as if they are entangled inside us. As we begin to heal, the force binding pain to love loses its grip. Slowly, the pain melts away and love fills its place.

This adjustment gets easier over time, especially when we help ourselves. So let's take some steps in that direction.

As children, we looked to our parents for emotional support. Now, it's our job to parent ourselves. How? By being present with our feelings without judging them. Let me explain.

Feelings have energy and are constantly moving like the current of a river. Some days that current is rippling; other times it's raging. The momentum varies depending on how we feel.

Problems arise when we stamp our feelings with disapproval because negative judgment acts like a dam. Instead of restricting the flow of water, it impairs our ability to process strong emotion.

The antidote to judgment is acceptance. I'm not referring to accepting the loss of a loved one. That will come in time. I am talking about accepting and honoring the way we feel about our loss.

Coping with Grief

When we were young, we cried anytime we felt like it, with no concern for who we were with, how red our faces got, or how far our voices carried. As grown-ups, we're generally not that uninhibited.

Even when we are grieving, some of us are uncomfortable expressing strong feelings. Maybe we are fighting back tears to avoid facing what happened. We could be afraid that once we start crying, we won't be able to stop. Or maybe, we consider displays of emotion a sign of weakness. Whatever the reason, whether it's judgment, avoidance, or fear – we are attempting to distance ourselves from our pain

Trying to keep from crying is like using the hold button on the telephone. When we put someone on hold, we can no longer hear their voice, but we are still connected. Likewise, when we choke back our tears, we're still connected to our pain. We are just resisting feeling it.

Resistance does not minimize our suffering. If anything, it amplifies it. And if it continues for too long, resistance can create problems of its own.

Here is what happens: When something impacts us unfavorably, we tighten up, we contract, we hold our breath. When we cry, we release the tension, the contraction, the tightening. This release helps restore the balance that was interrupted by whatever brought on the tears in the first place.

Crying may not heal our distress in an instant, but it does provide some relief. It also helps us get in touch with our emotions, which is a necessary part of the healing process.

Facing our feelings falls under the category of befriending ourselves. That is the sweetest medicine around and a reliable way to keep our lives afloat when we're adapting to change.

Sanctuary

On the following pages, I would like to invite you to take part in a healing exercise. If your emotions intensify, try leaning into your feelings, rather than pushing them away.

We will begin by inhaling and exhaling through the nose. Breathe in deeply, then exhale. That's good. Slowly inhale, then exhale. Keep going. Inhale, then exhale. Continue taking slow, deep, even breaths.

Next, picture a beautiful door in front of you. Turn the imaginary doorknob and walk inside.

The room is well lit and tastefully decorated in a rainbow of soft hues. Two comfortable looking easy chairs sit facing one another. Take a seat in one of them, and feel the weight of your body sink into thick cushions that provide support in all the right places.

Take another deep breath through the nose. This time, tense your shoulders as you inhale. Relax them as you exhale. Again, inhale and tense your shoulders. Exhale and relax your shoulders. Well done.

Visualize two strong hands kneading away the tension in your lower back. Feel them traveling up your spine, massaging your upper back, your neck, your ears and scalp, coming around to your temples and softly letting go.

If you are inclined, with the tips of your fingers, apply slight pressure to your eyebrows, starting at the bridge of your nose and working outwards towards your ears. Then relax your hands.

Feeling more at ease, think about how you and the deceased felt about each other. Remember their laughter. Recall the sound of their voice. Take a few minutes to savor these memories. They represent finely spun threads connecting your soul to theirs.

Picture your dear one standing in front of you. With that image in place, call their name. Invite him or her to take a seat, gesturing to the empty chair.

You may feel the need for closure. There could be things you never voiced, feelings you only got in touch with after they passed. Take this time to communicate with them as honestly as you can. Speak openly, without holding back.

Were you afraid for them or afraid for yourself? Maybe you weren't sure you could manage without them. Share those feelings. Or talk about how their life impacted yours and how you benefitted from knowing them. If you would like to thank them or express your love, do it now.

Take it easy. There is no rush, no timetable, no pressure to say it all at once. The two of you share a spiritual bond. You can resume this conversation at will.

It is very likely you did not want them to leave. Are you beginning to see there may have been other forces at play besides the obvious?

After you have spoken, nod to indicate that it's their turn to speak. They say:

"I am in a familiar place, where I feel safe and loved and cared for. To you, it may seem like something has ended. For me, something has begun anew. I learned so much from knowing you, and I continue to learn and grow.

"I'm nearby. You can call me. You can talk to me. When I hear you, I will lean real close and whisper in your ear to remind you how precious you are and how vital it is to honor your life.

"Let people meet the real you. Look into their eyes when you speak so they can see you the same way I see you – the way you are without any effort. Just be natural with your feelings. That is the truth of who you are."

As your dear one's voice gently fades, thank him or her for coming. Take another slow breath through your nose. Sit up straighter in your chair, and open your mind to the idea of trusting more.

Can you feel the weight on your heart start to lift and the space between your ears and your shoulders increase? Does your breathing feel lighter and less constricted?

Are you starting to see that having a full, rich, happy life is not irreverent? Holding on to the pain is. You can go forward from here feeling freer, and calmer, and strengthened from within.

Next, lace your fingers together and shake hands with yourself, sealing an agreement to stay in touch with your feelings. Then stand up, stretch, and walk though the door with renewed possibilities.

Although you just left the room, you can return to it whenever you want to. Everyone deserves to have a sanctuary. This one is yours alone, so it has to be someplace private. I know, let's create the room in your heart and put the door in your awareness. That way, you can find it easily.

Be creative. Enhance the room to reflect your personal taste, or recreate it whenever you go there. Fill it with fragrant flowers, or paint the walls your favorite color. Add a window overlooking a garden in full bloom or a turquoise lake with a waterfall.

You could even make the door an entrance to an entirely new domain bursting with colors, and bird song, and perpetual sunshine.

This is your own personal retreat. A place where you can meet yourself and cry openly, bringing you the relief you deserve. Here you can convene with your loved ones or commune with your own soul. Drawing courage from the on-going parlay between your heaven-self and your earth-self, as the breath we call life tenderly binds one to another.

Souls don't wear watches.
You can talk to your loved one any time.

Ceremony

Ceremony plays a part in every culture. Funerals offer closure as well as a sense of fellowship. Being with others who relate to how we feel can be very nurturing.

These gatherings allow us to pay tribute to our loved ones – to thank them, and praise them, and tell them how much they mean to us. While it may not eclipse the grief we feel, focusing on the positive is elevating to all concerned. It sends an empowering message to those who have passed, affirming their life had meaning.

For the memorial, I opt for raw honesty without pretense or politeness. Try passing the microphone around so everyone gets a turn to speak. Have someone introduce the idea ahead of time to help people relax. Tell them to talk freely and openly. Encourage them to speak from the heart. It does not have to sound polished or original.

Rather than talking about the deceased, try talking to them. I think you will find it more satisfying.

If the memorial has already passed, that's okay. Souls do not wear watches or measure time the way we do. You can talk to your dear one anytime of the day or night.

Life is so tentative it can be altered in a moment, yet full of promise and potential. As well as paying tribute to the people we care about, funerals give us an opportunity to reflect on our own lives, and ask ourselves if the choices we're making are aligned with our deepest desires.

Preparing to Depart

Until this point, we have been discussing how to cope with grief. Let's take a slight detour and discuss what happens before the funeral, when a loved one is preparing to depart. Following are a few insights you may find useful:

Illness rarely comes at convenient times. When it's life-threatening, it's natural to feel apprehensive. Consumed by a mixture of emotions, some of us don't know if we can handle watching a dear one wane. If you've ever been in this situation, you will probably agree with what I am about to say.

Each of us possesses an inner strength and the ability to access it. If you are willing to support your loved one through this difficult time, that strength will rise up to meet you. You'll discover the patience and endurance you need – as though a vault opens inside you, revealing a generous supply of love and the power love brings.

41

When Souls Take Flight

This is more than a poetic phrase. Love is a viable force that will empower you when you let it. You can draw energy from love the same way you withdraw money from the bank, with one notable difference. You can take out as much as you want, and your account always stays full.

Caregiving

Caring for someone during their final hours can be rewarding and provide a sense of closure. It can be therapeutic and transform your entire outlook. It can also be demanding and exhausting, both physically and emotionally.

Ideally, family members share caregiving responsibilities equally. As we know, that's not always the case. They frequently fall on a few willing shoulders.

If those shoulders happen to be yours, try not to ignore your own needs in the process. Too often, when someone else's are so immediate, ours get put on the back burner.

If you are not one of the primary caregivers, I urge you to find room in your heart, your schedule, and if need be, your wallet, to support whoever is shouldering the greatest responsibility. Instead of waiting for them to ask for help, consider offering it from your side.

There is freedom in forgiveness.

Forgiveness

Let's discuss easing your loved one's transition. Regardless of what your relationship has been in the past, especially if there has been some kind of conflict or misunderstanding, this is a chance for you to demonstrate kindness and compassion. You may think you are doing it for their sake, but you'll both benefit.

If your dear one is able to converse, encourage him or her to talk. If they are hesitant, take the lead. Ask them questions about their lives. Ask about the people they loved and their happiest memories. Ask them about the challenges they faced and how they overcame them. Ask anything that comes to mind. There may be a subject you would like to hear more about.

Take a genuine interest in what they're saying. Let them know that you are willing to listen for as long as they feel like talking.

The outcome might surprise you. You may find the two of you may have more in common than you realized. Recognizing similarities clears the way for more love to flow.

At your own pace, join in and make it a two-way conversation. Dig deep and be as forthright as you can. Suggest they do the same. This way, neither of you will feel there is anything left unsaid.

Something that may come up during these talks are unresolved feelings towards others or criticism of oneself. While we cannot tell another person how to feel, we can expound on the value of forgiveness. Tell your dear one forgiveness will help ease their burdens.

What if they say they did something unforgivable? Ask them if they want to talk about it. And if they do, see if you can listen without judging them. That in itself can facilitate healing.

What if they feel the need to have others forgive them? Ask how they would feel about talking to that person (or persons) now.

What if you cannot get in touch with them? Is there a way to communicate with someone who isn't present? Yes, there is. We can speak to someone who is not present through the heart. Let me explain.

We can liken our hearts to a magical tree and our feelings to its branches. Why is it magical? Because those branches can travel. Take love for example. It can travel through telephone wires, through walls, through space, across oceans. Love can even travel from one dimension to another, one soul to another.

Tailor the following exercise to suit the needs of the individual you're trying to assist. If he or she feels the need to forgive someone, have them picture the individual or individuals they need to forgive. If they feel the need to be forgiven by someone, have them picture that individual (s). If they feel the need for self-forgiveness, tell them to picture their own image to dialogue with. Then, in a relaxed voice read these instructions out loud:

"Close your eyes. Take a few slow, gentle breaths. See yourself face to face with the person or persons you want to speak to. That's good. They are standing directly in front of you. Notice how your heart and his or her heart are also facing one another.

"Silently speak from your heart to their heart. Be direct, and talk openly and honestly. Empty yourself. Say everything you feel the need to say.

"If you want to forgive them, go ahead. Forgive them. If you want to apologize, apologize. If you want to ask for forgiveness, ask for forgiveness. If you want to forgive yourself, forgive yourself. This is a perfect time to make peace with the past."

Can the person (s) they are talking to hear them? I would like to think they can. What's really important is the intention behind their words. There is freedom in forgiving others, freedom in taking responsibility for our actions and acknowledging our wrongdoing, freedom in asking someone for forgiveness, and freedom in forgiving ourselves.

Does it work? Does apologizing and asking for forgiveness automatically erase one's misconduct and wipe the slate clean? Maybe not, but the humility in a sincere apology is a great place to start.

Isn't it too late for new beginnings? Who said life ends when the soul leaves the body?

Honoring

Earlier, I said a divine event takes place when someone dies. Then it stands to reason, when someone is preparing to depart, a holy or divine event is about to take place.

Facing death can provoke some turbulent feelings. Typically, the ambiance in the home or hospital room of a dying person is one of foreboding, rather than reverence. Does it have to be?

Sometimes death comes quickly and leaves little time to prepare. Other times we see it approaching. This allows us to provide a heartwarming send-off. Wouldn't you like being pampered if you were the one lying in that bed?

Create a pleasing, tranquil environment. Open the curtains. Position the bed so they can see the sky. Put pictures of family members and friends within reach. Surround them with their favorite mementos. Play their favorite music. Serve their favorite foods.

If they like essential oils, get an aromatherapy pot or a diffuser and fill the room with delicious scents. (A word of caution, use natural aromas only.)

See to their comfort. If they are having visitors, they may not want to be in their bedclothes when people arrive. Perhaps they would like help getting dressed, or want to have their hair done, or even get a manicure and pedicure. If they do, try to arrange it. Call a local salon to see if they provide home services, or if they know someone who does.

This may sound frivolous to some of us, but we are not here to judge. We are here to support and be of service. How? By honoring our dear one's desires. What are they? We won't know unless we ask.

On another subject, why wait for the memorial to gather friends and family to sing their praise? We often hear these moving stories told at memorials and question whether or not the deceased can hear what is being said about them. Why not say it when we are sure they can hear us? Love and gratitude make the best going away presents.

Needless to say, proceed with respect and comply with your dear one's wishes. This is not about what you want for them. It is about what they want for themselves. If they prefer to be alone, by all means give them their space.

Parting Words

People take their beliefs about death seriously. A person could be moments away from realizing their divine nature and still be afraid. Fear of dying stems from fear of the unknown and the belief our lives are limited to the physical body.

Reading the following points aloud may soften these beliefs and the fear they trigger. To highlight the main points, I have repeated some of the ideas already presented.

Read the text the way it's written, or put it in your own words. Either way, be gentle and try to convey a feeling of comfort. In a clear voice, say:

"You are strong. You only feel weak because your body is getting ready to retire. But you are not your body. You never were. You are a soul, a custodian, a guardian, endowed with this physical form so you can experience being human.

"The relationship you have with your body isn't permanent. It's temporary because the physical body is mortal. Your soul is immortal, so you will not die when your body subsides. You have a long life ahead of you.

"When your breathing stills, you'll have a deeply satisfying moment. Your soul will easily disengage from your body. And any pain or discomfort, any physical disability or impairment will be instantly lifted. You will feel exalted and liberated.

"You may be under the impression that your mind will go blank when this happens. That is a big misconception. Souls are aware and have their own intelligence. They are capable of remembering, deciding, reasoning, discerning, etc. These are only a few of the abilities which came with you when you arrived and will go with you when you depart. Your consciousness goes wherever you go.

"Some people believe that you will be encased in darkness when you die. This is another inaccuracy. Your soul is lit from within, and that light is a spark of divinity shining through you. It is steady and unwavering. Like your consciousness, it goes wherever you go.

Parting Words

"People say you cannot take anything with you when you die, but you can. You are allowed to take one large suitcase, and it is already packed full of feelings and memories.

"If you're wondering who is going to carry that suitcase, your soul has a body of its own. It's lighter and more mobile than your physical one, which is why it is called a light body.

"The word 'light' has two meanings. It can refer to a measure of weight or a measure of brightness. Where the soul is concerned, it's both light enough to float and luminous.

"You may be feeling tired right now, and your mind may be hazy. That will pass. Soon, you will feel fresh and vibrant enough to appreciate the wonder and beauty of what you are about to experience.

"Take a few moments to picture the afterlife. Let your mind roam freely. See yourself in an enchanting, relaxed atmosphere, where you are surrounded by loved ones. Picture it looking and feeling as glorious as you always hoped it would be. When you arrive, it will be more sublime and pleasing than anything you envisioned.

"If you have concerns about knowing where to go once your soul departs, you can relax. You won't be wandering the spiritual highway looking for a way in. You will be guided to a specific location, where the familiar faces of family and friends will be eagerly waiting to greet you. They may even throw a party in your honor.

"If you have any questions about where you are, or where you are going, or what's happening to you, feel free to ask for help. You will be surprised by how quickly it arrives.

"You're about to embark on a mystical journey. Soon, you'll awaken from the dream of your earthly life, and discover the reality of your soul life. In an instant, you will see yourself as the sparkling being you truly are. In an instant, you will remember what it feels like to be free.

"It does not hurt to let go. It brings great relief. It only hurts to hold on.

"Listen to your soul. Trust what you know to be true. You are a sacred child, and nature is calling you home. So ready yourself to be bathed in the light of pure love."

Parting Words

Caregivers, assure your dear one that you'll be fine and so will they. Repeat the points you just read, especially the part about their upcoming journey. Remind them they will be reunited with their loved ones. Remind them they will be received with open arms.

Read to them from this book in its entirety. They may be skeptical at first, then ask you to repeat certain passages and draw solace from them. Follow their lead.

The two realms are forever connected
in a seamless dance of communion.

Communion

As your dear one begins to withdraw from this world and ready themselves for the next, you may notice some changes in their behavior.

They may talk about, or talk to, deceased relatives and friends. It could be someone they haven't seen or mentioned in years. This is fairly common. Even family members report having an increased awareness of those who have passed.

Do you remember when I said seeing my father depart was like watching a train pull away from the station? Well, your dear one is about to get on that train, and those souls are probably on the platform waiting to receive them. If you were meeting someone after a trip, wouldn't you call ahead to let them know you were coming?

There is another behavior you might observe. You may see your loved one stare into space with a fixed gaze. To explain why this happens, I'd like to tell you about an event that took place at the bedside of a close friend. Her eyes were open, and she appeared to be looking at something only she could see. Watching her, I had the distinct impression her body was in one place and her mind was in another.

This is how I see it. When someone is close to departing, their consciousness weaves between the physical realm (of the body) and the spiritual realm (of the soul) in a continuous loop like an infinity sign, until the soul makes its final departure. Even then, the two realms remain unified. Indivisible. Forever connected in a seamless dance of communion.

Soul to Soul

Before we talk about the final hours, I would like to address a concern shared by many. What if we are unable to be at the bedside of someone we love when they depart? Can we still say goodbye?

Well-meaning friends try to assure us we can, and they are absolutely right. As soul-based beings, we have the ability to communicate with other souls. Think of it as an internal cell phone charged by the divine. All we do is go within, call our loved one, and speak from the heart.

Divinity waits with open arms.

The Golden Hour

Close to departing, your dear one may appear to be in a trance-like sleep. They may be non-responsive and seem unaware of your presence. Try not to make assumptions. It is very likely they do know you are there, but they cannot express it outwardly.

Continue to lovingly address their needs. Keep them clean and comfortable. Make sure the room is well ventilated. Play soft music. Hold his or her hand. Talk or sit quietly. Know with absolute certainty that your presence has meaning.

Once your loved one takes their final breath, keep speaking to them. Be positive, even if you are crying. Crying is a natural release. So let those tears come.

Thank them. Praise them. Sing or sit in silence. Pray if you feel moved to. Say and do anything and everything you are called to do, and know that it is perfect.

When Souls Take Flight

Whenever you feel ready, walk over to a mirror. Look into your eyes, and assure yourself you will get through this. You have witnessed the ebb and flow of life, and even if your mind tries to convince you that something tragic has occurred, something profoundly beautiful has taken place.

The physical body has come to rest, and light as a song, the soul has taken flight.

From Beyond

This message is for you ....

"I am to you that which you are to me because if my death touched you and stirred your heart, I rest easy knowing my life also touched you.

"Some of us leave fingerprints and some leave footprints. Whether my years with you were few or many – whether my departure was sudden and unexpected, or drawn out and anticipated – whether I died from an accident, a fatal disease, or the grace of old age – whether my life was taken by another or by my own hand – whether I went peacefully or resisted, I was not alone. Not then and not now.

"If you miss seeing me, if you miss my touch or the sound of my voice, feel me as I am. As near to you as the salt is to the sea.

"If you suffer over not having spent more time with me, if you're saddened from not having been there when I passed, know that you are with me now.

"If you find yourself reliving your own idea of what my parting moments were like and are claiming my pain as your own, I invite you to lay down your concerns at the feet of my memory.

"If you are struggling to keep from crying, let me hold you as you surrender to the cleansing your tears will bring.

"There is so much confusion around dying, so many misunderstood perceptions. My soul is as alive to me as yours is to you. Death is not the absence of life. It is merely the absence of the physical form.

"I know now what I had forgotten. The breath may have left my body, but the love has not left my heart. You and I live on eternally within each other. Every time you think of me, I am here."

Loving Gratitude

Samuel and Beatrice Rosner, Michael Rosner, Tim Shea, Jim Fairchild, Dannion and Kathryn Brinkley, Pianta, Connie and Jim Newton, Monte Walker, Louise Burgan, June d'Estelle, Peter Navarro, Carole Glenn, Gail Stein, Dawn Lianna, Kate O'Rielly, Darrell and Edith Durfey, Caroline Sutherland and Gary Leikas, Oshara Helton, Frances Allden and Sid Smither, Jean and Jon Iverson, Winalee and Ron Zeeb, Marty Broda, Bonnie Frenkel, Denise Medved and Roger Belford, Mary Stevenson, Gerri Scharf, Barbara Schwartz, Marilyn Carr, Jan Stevens, Bob and Judy Bernards, Catherine Lyons, Bill Graham, Paul Cohen, Tim and Michelle Campbell, Audra Stone, Rodney and Nandini Charles, Gary and Janet Halprin, Girish and Asha Srivastava, Mrs. Sharma, Advid Sharma, Ghanshyan and Prem Gupta, Patti Gordon, Savitri Vidya, George Bresler, Alan and Melanie Shapiro-Kornfield, Sylvia Eskenazi, Maimie Rittenband, Abraham Rutman, Neil and Alice Grossman, Edward and Helen Mitchell, Beverly and Jay May, Debbie Marshall, Bobby Pisano, Evelyn Lax, Alfred and Doris Schwartz, John Giblin, Michael Albright, Barry Whitfield, my beloved friends and family around the globe. I value your presence in my life.

When Souls Take Flight:
Coping with Grief
Kira Rosner

Available At Your Favorite Bookstores
Online & Off

Print: ISBN 978-0-9679978-2-7
eBook: ISBN 978-0-9679978-1-0

www.WhenSoulsTakeFlight.com

Also by Kira Rosner

The Power of Being Human

"You are a valuable, deserving being. If you believe otherwise, the fault is in your thinking – not in you."
Kira Rosner

Human beings are innately powerful. Our lives are a reflection of how we express that power. With light banter and easy-to-understand prose, this uplifting guide sweetens the idea that many of us repress our power instead of expressing it.

What is the remedy? A healing technique which integrates three of the most powerful forces in the universe.

Available At Your Favorite Bookstores
Online & Off

Print: ISBN 978-0-9679978-5-8
eBook: ISBN 978-0-9679978-6-5

www.KiraRosner.com

Also by Kira Rosner

Taking the Longing Out of Belonging

"Belonging is the divine maternal instinct spread like jam throughout a universe of diversity."

Kira Rosner

You and I are stewards for this sacred triad of heart, mind, and body. Will you look beyond the peel to the fruit, where our soul and body renew their vows – promising to love, honor, and cherish one another in luminescent shades of synergy?

Imagine if feeling good was not dependent on outside circumstances. Yes, imagine.

Available At Your Favorite Bookstores
Online & Off

Print: ISBN: 978-0-9679978-3-4
eBook: ISBN: 978-0-9679978-4-1

www.KiraRosner.com

Books by Kira Rosner

The Power of Being Human
Taking the Longing Out of Belonging
When Souls Take Flight: Coping with Grief

*These books share a common thread
and may contain similar excerpts.

www.KiraRosner.com

www.ingramcontent.com/pod-product-compliance
Lightning Source LLC
Chambersburg PA
CBHW031330040426
42443CB00005B/285

* 9 7 8 0 9 6 7 9 9 7 8 2 7 *